LOOK

SARA MAYA WEBB

BookLeaf Publishing

India | USA | UK

Presentation by *BookLeaf Publishing*

Web: www.bookleafpub.com

E-mail: info@bookleafpub.com

ISBN: 978-93-95088-86-2

First edition 2022

DEDICATION

For Liliana, Grace, Julia, all womxn

ACKNOWLEDGEMENTS

Warm appreciation to Susie Darin and
Allison Nolen.
Carla ~ I could not have published a word
without your love and support.

PREFACE

The author recommends reading these
works in the order they are presented.

Elixir

Sip these words
Roll them around on the tongue
of your mind

Allow each syllable
to slowly tumble down
to rumble

Bathe In these words
allow them to marinate
So the subconscious
can bubble
up

Make space
for new ideas to
nestle near
your soul

Transmute your creation
Allow
your higher Self to
Heal

Seek

Looking is much more
than
seeing

Looking is much less
than
SEEKING

Seek truth, for freedom
can be found
~

At this
very moment
at any moment
at every moment

the one person
who can change
your life
infinitely
indefinitely
is
you

But first
do
not
look
away

Data Processor

billions of bits of data
are always
around us

the human brain gobbles
approximately
11 million bits
per second

but

we are aware of roughly
45 bits
of the 11 million

most of the data
our bodies ingest are
subconscious

we can only
consciously look at
.04%
of reality
each instant

here begin our gut feelings
and
feeling things in our bones
and
hair standing up
on backs of our necks

Reactions

instead of dissociation
or distraction

Look at the root
Anger
Sadness
Fear

Find the original trauma
but don't get stuck

flow ~ flow ~ flow
instead of
focus

Sometimes we laugh for minutes on end
until we cannot
breathe
giggle until tears trickle

but
for big work
it may take
years of tears
until
we inhale
fully
and can belly laugh
again

Heal

Living with intention
demands
observation of our lives from
above

It requires looking carefully
at the things
we
don't
want to
perpetuate

Consciously unpeeling
layers
of perception
and
applying an upgraded
lens
to our chosen reality

First
we look
at the wound
however old it may be
hear its tales
by walking along its lines
until we are able to see
a scar
as utter beauty

Perception

Looks are ephemeral

and

only as we grow old
do we have
the unique opportunity
to choose to grow
more beautiful

I choose
to look for
and
appreciate
the Good
the Beauty
the Joy

Looking for Healing

the men who raped me
could have easily held me down
with
that
many
hands
but they used a drug
anyway

the physical wounds
have long ago
healed

Now looking at the rage
sitting in the sting
I feel a little heal
I see a seed
to grow

Roar

I could not
have told
the man who held me at 8 minutes old
Looked, then said
he'd fight a lion for me

I thought I could not have told
the police
for
the perps had silenced my throat
used it for glee
rendering me powerless
leaving bruises for memories

I could not have told another soul, save my
24-year old
Sister
for the guilt I embodied
for the fear I'd be shunned
for the shame I'd be blamed

I speak about it now
not just to heal myself
not only to protect my daughters

but for the millions of womxn
still afraid to say
me too

Metamorphosis

They shushed my voicebox
along with my consciousness
several short hours
of my then-27-year old life

They tried to defile the box
between my legs
boxed
my face
propped me
outside a lobby
to wake at dawn

as I was last to learn of my fate
I squelched myself to silence
boxed my brain between
flimsy fences of foreboding humiliation

until I became
the
box

Oh, how that box served me.
Triage unit, initially
Chrysalis, finally

splutter-to-flutter
I raise my winged voice
so we all
can rise

Stardust

Looking within arouses
fear

Most people resist
petrified
of what they will find but

quantum physics says we are
unadulterated energy
sheer space
pure possibility

every cell
is
starlight

continue to peer
gaze deeper
within

pure potentiality
materializes

Midst of a Trigger

Look at the trauma
trite or tough

allow the
very next
look
to be the
emotions triggered
by
same similar events

Healing begins
when
whimper
becomes
waltz

Emotions

We can see something without intention
but to look
requires desire

magnifying glass
reveals that
FEAR
rules

Fear is the foe of Love – its precise
opposite

Anger
is
fear
every iteration of it
resentment to rage
and all between

Sadness
is
fear – just look
at the ultimate
sadness:
grief

stripped down
is it not
fear
of coping
without
our dear loved
one

Guilt
plays variously
dressed up
assorted blends
of anger, fear, sadness

Look for the love

Find yourself
in love with your life

Restoration

To heal body mind soul

get the gunk out
let it ooze
from your pores
yoga walk run yourself

Sit down
to practice
autonomic writing

pranayama through it

Breathe, intentionally, in provocative,
methodical ways

Look to the ancients

Meditate
Meditate ~ Meditate
~ ~ ~
meditate some more

Ask
out Loud
for Divine assistance

Embody these practices

You don't need a grand plan

Just do
the
next right
thing

Words Have Weight

Change the way

you look at

obstacles

for

they are

springboards

Healing from the
Body Shock
has propelled me
to new limits
of
Strength

Meditation

We
have

5 senses

11 million sensory
receptors
in our bodies

10 million of them
are dedicated to
sight

When we close our eyes
we are better able to perceive
that which lies within

to look at that
which
the light
does
not
touch

Magic

Manifesting is the most
beautiful form
of self-delusion

It is consciously choosing
to accept
only the reality
of our creation

Contemplation

Silence allows us to
look

Find time
Make time
Get quiet

Sit with eyes closed
Listen to the body

Patience

becomes

awareness

Carla

She
fills
spaces

inside
me

inside
my
broken
healing
heart

where
I never
knew
to
look

Take a Chance

Freedom

often

looks like

danger

Follow the Beam

Look toward the
Light

to see the
Good

the Light within
you

the Light around
you

the Light

that

is

you

Keys to Enlightenment

Look
for the
Good

Find
the
Joy

Fall
in
Love
with your own rich magnificence

E x p a n d
into
what you find

Your healing is inside
close your eyes
and
Look

www.ingramcontent.com/pod-product-compliance
Lightning Source LLC
Chambersburg PA
CBHW061321140726
47998CB00006B/2496